ESTÉE
LAUDER

Businesswoman and Cosmetics Pioneer

ESTÉE
LAUDER

Businesswoman and Cosmetics Pioneer

BY ROBERT GRAYSON

CONTENT CONSULTANT
TRACEY DEUTSCH
ASSOCIATE PROFESSOR OF HISTORY
UNIVERSITY OF MINNESOTA

ABDO
Publishing Company

CREDITS

Published by ABDO Publishing Company, PO Box 398166, Minneapolis, MN 55439. Copyright © 2014 by Abdo Consulting Group, Inc. International copyrights reserved in all countries. No part of this book may be reproduced in any form without written permission from the publisher. The Essential Library™ is a trademark and logo of ABDO Publishing Company.

Printed in the United States of America,
North Mankato, Minnesota
052013
092013

 THIS BOOK CONTAINS AT LEAST 10% RECYCLED MATERIALS.

Editor: Arnold Ringstad
Series Designer: Becky Daum

Photo credits: AP Images, cover, 2, 59; Jennifer Graylock/AP Images, 6; Ray Fisher/ Time Life Pictures/Getty Images, 10; Abe Fox/AP Images, 14; AuthenticatedNews/ Getty Images, 16; Mario Ruiz/Time Life Pictures/Getty Images, 22; CTK/AP Images, 24; Jim Henderson, 26; Irv Steinberg/Globe Photos, 29; Steve Finn/Alpha/Globe Photos, 33; Bill Sauro/New York World Journal Tribune/Library of Congress, 34; Luo Yunfei/Imagechina/AP Images, 39; Gerald Herbert/AP Images, 43, 82; Jim Wells/AP Images, 44; Alfred Eisenstaedt/Time & Life Pictures/Getty Images, 48; Mark Lennihan/ AP Images, 52; Ron Galella/WireImage/Getty Images, 54; Christophe Ena/AP Images, 61; Business Wire/Getty Images, 62; Evening Standard/Getty Images, 64; Frazer Harrison/Getty Images, 68; PRNewsFoto/AP Images, 72; PRNewsFoto/Clinique/AP Images, 74, 79; Tom Gates/Getty Images, 84; Susan Ragan/AP Images, 89; Ron Galella/ WireImage/Getty Images, 92; Rose Hartman/Getty Images, 94

Library of Congress Control Number: 2013932921

Cataloging-in-Publication Data

Grayson, Robert.
 Estee Lauder : businesswoman and cosmetics pioneer / Robert Grayson.
   p. cm. -- (Essential lives)
ISBN 978-1-61783-892-7
Includes bibliographical references and index.
1. Lauder, Estee--Juvenile literature. 2. Estee Lauder, Inc.--History--Juvenile literature. 3. Cosmetics industry--United States--Biography--Juvenile literature. 4. Perfumes industry--United States--Biography--Juvenile literature. 5. Businesswomen--United States--Biography--Juvenile literature. I. Title.
338.7/092--dc23
[B]   2013932921

CONTENTS

CHAPTER
ONE

YOUTH DEW

In the world of fragrances, words such as *warm*, *feminine*, *refined*, and *classic* are still used to describe the iconic perfume known as Youth Dew. It took the cosmetics industry by storm upon its introduction by Estée Lauder in 1953. This sensory sensation established Lauder's company as a powerhouse in the highly competitive beauty industry.

Lauder had worked hard to establish a foothold in the beauty business. She got her start in the 1930s selling skin care products in New York City, New York, beauty salons. She developed the products with the help of her uncle, a chemist named John Schotz, who shared her interest in skin care.

Lauder began selling her product line in some of the nation's most prestigious department stores, including Saks Fifth Avenue and Neiman Marcus, during the late 1940s. Space was usually reserved for big, established cosmetics companies. But Lauder marketed her products with flair, letting customers try a product before

Youth Dew helped transform Estée Lauder from an ordinary businesswoman into a beauty industry icon.

purchasing it and showing them how to use it. Her creative and relentless promotional work convinced department-store executives to give Lauder counter space. Her business grew steadily as a result.

By the early 1950s, she was ready to put her marketing talents to the test again, this time by expanding her cosmetics line from skin care into fragrances. Years earlier, Lauder had worked on a fragrance with her uncle, but it had to be perfected before she could sell it to the public. She experimented

A TRUE NOSE

Nose is the term used to refer to a professional perfumer. It is a great compliment in the perfume world to be called a *true nose*. A true nose can tell the difference between a mediocre scent and a great one. Some believe true noses are born and cannot be taught. A person can train to become a nose, but to be truly great an uncanny sensitivity to fragrances is a must. A nose must be able to pick up any scents within range. Noses can distinguish between thousands of scents and can determine the components of a particular fragrance. Noses must be creative and have wonderful imaginations so they can develop the next great fragrance. They must have the ability to know which scents work well together and tweak them to discover new sensory delights. The process can sometimes take years.

Estée Lauder was considered a true nose. In the 1980s, Ernest Shifton, the chief perfumer of the renowned International Flavors and Fragrances in New York City, was attending an international perfumers convention in Paris. He proclaimed at the conference, "In all America, there is only one true nose and it belongs to Estée Lauder."[1]

with various essences, seeking to capture exactly the right scent.

Her reputation for testing her own products on herself until she was happy with them was legendary. "I've tried a product for years before I even talk about it to say it's good. I put it on my face until I haven't any face. I've taken enough baths—sometimes four in a row to try the bath gel—and I've put the cream on, and I take it off, and then half an hour later put it on again," she told beauty editors at *Vogue* magazine.[2] The painstaking work paid off. With Youth Dew, she had created a product that would propel her company to the next level. It would make Estée Lauder a household name across the country.

Scent of a Woman

In the mid 1900s, most perfumes were expensive.

MAKING SCENTS

Developing a fragrance seemed like the logical next step for Estée Lauder. Beauty moguls Helena Rubinstein and Elizabeth Arden, two of the biggest names in the beauty industry, both started with skin care products. They expanded their customer base by developing perfumes. Rubinstein and Arden had both been in business since the early 1900s, some 30 years before Lauder entered the fray. When Rubinstein and Arden launched their fragrances, neither enjoyed the success Lauder did with her signature fragrance. Youth Dew made Rubinstein and Arden realize Estée Lauder was a serious competitor in the beauty business.

In order to break into the beauty industry, Lauder knew she had to change the way people thought about perfumes.

Fragrances were usually imported from a foreign country, such as France, and used by women only on special occasions. The rest of the time, the classic scents would sit unused in a fancy bottle on a woman's dresser. For the most part, men purchased perfume for women as gifts. Very few women bought an expensive, high-end fragrance for themselves. Fragrances were considered a luxury.

For Lauder, the dilemma was clear. Perfume was the perfect romantic gift. "That was killing it," she recalled with a trace of irony.[3] The fact that people bought it so infrequently meant that business possibilities were lackluster. Lauder wanted to change this by developing a high-end perfume women felt comfortable buying for themselves and using on a daily basis. The cosmetics entrepreneur wanted to liberate the fragrance market from the perception that perfume was only for special occasions. But, like a good scent, her approach could not be overbearing.

With her fragrance perfected, Lauder decided to market it as bath oil that doubled as a perfume. Because the scent came from bath oil, women would not have to worry that wearing it during the day would give them an aura of extravagance in the way ordinary perfume would.

Youth Dew Debuts

Lauder's customers felt they could buy her scent as an everyday product, like lipstick. It was something that could be splashed on daily. She called her new scent Youth Dew. Best of all, the product was relatively affordable. Youth Dew sold

THE PROCESS

Developing a fragrance is extremely difficult. Those with the gift often say they can visualize the scent as well as smell it. "So palpable was a beautiful scent that I could see a splendid aura around the women who wore it," Lauder said.[4] After Youth Dew was launched, it took 15 years for Lauder to finally complete work on another scent. This one was called Estée. Lauder said she needed the time to truly understand all the nuances of this new fragrance.

for approximately $5.00 a bottle. Some perfumes sold by other beauty companies cost more than ten times as much.

Besides its price, Youth Dew sported another innovation. It did not come with a sealed cap on the bottle, as competitive products did. Youth Dew customers could twist off the cap and smell the scent in the store before buying it. Lauder always had unshakable confidence in her products, and it was no different with Youth Dew. She felt certain if women took just a whiff of Youth Dew, the product would sell itself.

The new bath oil was introduced at one of New York City's most glamorous department stores, Bonwit Teller, in 1953. The East Coast went crazy for Youth Dew. It did not take long for the product to make its way across the rest of the country, where it continued to sell well. To women across the United States, Youth Dew provided great value for their hard-earned money.

Lauder wore the scent everywhere. In stores where she had cosmetics counters, she applied it all over the place, even in the elevators. Women came looking for what was to become Estée Lauder's signature scent.

A Phenomenon

Youth Dew was an instant hit, dramatically boosting the sales of all Estée Lauder products. No other beauty company came close to the company's sales in the 1950s. Youth Dew became a phenomenon, and it is still popular today.

Lauder later used the bath oil to create spinoff products. She developed Youth Dew deodorant, hand lotion, cologne, perfume, and even body powder. All these products sold very well, with Lauder's marketing genius powering sales. At first, few advertising dollars were spent promoting Youth Dew. Instead, Lauder traveled across the country to department store cosmetics counters. Once there, her friendly and caring—yet passionate, enthusiastic, and skillful—style of selling had customers lining up to buy the product.

GOING HOLLYWOOD

Youth Dew had its share of well-known admirers. During an interview, movie star Joan Crawford mentioned she attracted her fourth husband by using it. Screen legend Gloria Swanson also told Hollywood reporters she used Youth Dew regularly. Actress Dolores Del Rio confessed she brushed it into her hair. Fashion designer Jo Copeland loved the way Youth Dew made her feel and was never shy about saying so.

By getting her products into upscale department stores, such as Bonwit Teller, Lauder associated her products with good taste and high fashion.

Samples Galore

Lauder persuaded many department stores to send out samples of Youth Dew on scented inserts with their bills or other mailings. Most of their customers had never received a scented mailer before. Many loved the fragrance and asked for the product the next time they came to the store.

Youth Dew became the foundation of the Estée Lauder line. Lauder's company quickly became a major player in the beauty industry. The product pushed Estée

Lauder sales far past those of entrenched cosmetics companies such as Charles of the Ritz and Dorothy Gray.

Youth Dew also propelled crossover sales. People who came to buy Youth Dew saw Lauder's skin care products and purchased those, too. In 1958, the company reached the milestone of $1 million in annual sales.[5] With the success of Youth Dew, Estée Lauder was poised to become a giant in the highly competitive international beauty business.

LOOKING GOOD

Lauder was good at marketing not just her products, but also herself. "There wasn't a minute of any day when I didn't look as pretty as I knew how to make myself. It was a matter of pride to me; it was a matter of self-respect. There was no reason ever to look sloppy because it takes so little time to look wonderful," she said.[6] And looking wonderful helped her sell, because the products making her look so good were the ones on her counter.

CHAPTER TWO

GROWING UP BEAUTIFUL

E stée Lauder, the daughter of Jewish immigrants, was born Josephine Esther Mentzer on July 1, 1908, in Queens, New York. Corona, the Queens neighborhood where Josephine grew up, was a mix of Italian and Jewish families. Her mother, Rose, was married twice. Rose was born in Hungary, where she married a cousin, Abraham Rosenthal. The couple had five children and decided to come to the United States in the late 1890s. Rose was 29 when she arrived in the United States with her children in August 1898.

Abraham Rosenthal had moved to the United States a few months earlier to pave the way for his family. But when Rose landed in New York City, her husband was not waiting for her at the pier. She never saw him again. As an adult, Lauder claimed to know little about her mother's first husband, saying her mother never talked about the marriage. Researchers have found scant trace

Few would have predicted young Josephine Esther Mentzer would grow up to become the rich and glamorous Estée Lauder.

of Rosenthal in historical records. No one in the family ever confirmed if he died upon his arrival in the United States, deserted the family, or secretly divorced Rose.

Once Rose and her children were settled in New York City, she married Max Mentzer, also a Hungarian immigrant, in approximately 1904. The exact date of the marriage is unknown; official records were never located. Max Mentzer was believed to be ten years younger than Rose. They had four children, but two

HER FATHER'S DISAPPROVAL

Max Mentzer was not happy with his daughter's obsession with making women's faces look beautiful. Josephine was convinced of her ability to create magic on any woman's face. She loved to see a woman with glowing skin, inviting lips, and mesmerizing eyes. Her father's response was to tell his eager daughter to "stop fiddling with other people's faces."[1] He never understood his daughter's fascination.

However, Josephine's second choice of career worried Mentzer even more. She confided in her father there were times she dreamed of being an actress and having her name in lights on Broadway. That was hardly out of the question for Josephine, especially because she had such radiant skin. She also had a good memory, essential for remembering lines in a script. Actresses were usually portrayed as beautiful and glamorous. They always wore the finest clothes and never had a single hair out of place as they waved to an adoring public. It was a life filled with much of the same excitement that attracted Josephine to the world of cosmetics.

died in infancy. The two survivors were Josephine and her older sister, Renee. They grew up with five older half siblings from Rose's first marriage.

Josephine's fascination with beauty and glamour began at an early age, when she first realized how interested many women were in looking good. As a youngster, she was captivated by her mother's determination to look youthful and ravishing. To her mother, style was nothing short of an art form.

"My mother began brushing her golden hair in the morning even before she opened her eyes," Lauder recalled in her autobiography.[2] She remembered her mother's beauty lessons as if they were chiseled in stone, including the most important: "You're as beautiful as you think you are."[3]

A New Name

Rose wanted her daughter's first name to be Esty, after one of Rose's favorite aunts. But a nurse friend encouraged her to use Esty as a middle name instead. The nurse recommended Rose name her daughter Josephine because it sounded more American. Rose agreed. When Josephine was born, the clerk who registered the birth had never heard of the name Esty and simply recorded the child's middle name as the more common Esther. Nevertheless, the Mentzers always called their youngest child Esty, and so did her friends.

When she was first enrolled in school, teachers were confused by the name Esty as well. Josephine tried out different names before finally settling on Estée, adding a French accent for a bit of European flavor. Estée liked it, and the name stuck.

Marketing Roots

When Estée's father, Max Mentzer, first came to America, he worked as a custom tailor who made clothes to order. However, he did not like the work, so he purchased a hardware store in Queens. The store was across the street from a department store, Plafker and Rosenthal. It was run by the Leppel sisters, Fannie and Frieda, and their husbands. Fannie's husband was Isidor Rosenthal, one of Estée's half brothers, so she was Estée's

GOOD IMPRESSION

As an impressionable youngster, Estée saw something during her time at Plafker and Rosenthal that many young girls of her day never did. She witnessed two strong, successful women in business. In her mind, it was not far-fetched to envision herself running a thriving business as well.

sister-in-law. Estée divided her time after school between the hardware store and the department store. Though she was young, she absorbed knowledge about sales and marketing in both retail settings. Watching how Fannie and Frieda interacted with their customers, she gained a keen understanding of how to persuade people to buy products.

Estée observed how Fannie and Frieda went out of their way to learn what their customers wanted and make sure the store stocked it. They extended credit to those who needed it. They spoke both Yiddish and Italian, making their customers feel welcome and comfortable in the store. The department store became a beloved retail destination in the neighborhood.

Learning from Fannie and Frieda, Estée made product displays at her father's hardware store more interesting so the merchandise would stand out more. She became friendly with many of the customers, listening

A LOVE FOR FASHION

Estée gained an appreciation for fine clothing while spending time at Plafker and Rosenthal. The department store carried chic fabrics and high-end clothing. Estée loved touching the elegantly woven material and trying on the clothes. Throughout her life, she maintained an interest in fashion and designer clothes, convinced quality cosmetics and fragrances complemented the perfect outfit.

Individualized service, taking each customer's unique needs into consideration, would be key to Estée's success.

to their concerns and providing helpful customer service. She developed a strong relationship with the customers and gave them lots of individual attention. These were lessons Estée never forgot as she built her cosmetics empire.

Estée's interest in beauty and cosmetics never waned. During her days at the department store, she would style Fannie's hair when both had spare time. She also enjoyed helping customers choose outfits for their children to wear to special events. She always paid careful attention to the appearance of her own skin, using her mother's face creams regularly. Estée, a petite blonde, was known in her neighborhood for her glowing skin.

Meeting Her Mentor

With her marketing education well under way, Estée met the person who would have the most profound impact on her life. Her mother's brother, John Schotz, came to live with the family after World War I (1914–1918). Schotz was a chemist who spent a great deal of time studying skin and inventing creams to keep it cleansed, nourished, and youthful looking.

Estée was ecstatic when she met her uncle. "He captured my imagination and interest as no one else ever had. . . . He understood me. What's more, he produced miracles," she said of Schotz.[4] Watching her uncle work made Estée realize the path she wanted to take in life. This bespectacled, brown-haired man with a fair complexion, who loved touching faces and making skin glow, was the answer to a prayer for Estée. He took her interest in beauty very seriously. He was living her dream, creating magic potions that changed women's looks. "That is what I'd like to do—touch people's faces, no matter who they were, touch them and make them pretty," she remembered.[5]

Even today, cosmetics are often designed in labs not unlike John Schotz's.

Schotz was equally pleased to find a member of the family who took an interest in what he did, and he was happy to share his knowledge with Estée. He built a small laboratory behind Estée's house to mix his products.

Estée soon started doing odd jobs around the lab for her uncle. For several years, she soaked up knowledge about everything she saw her uncle do in the lab. In her late teens, she began mixing batches of her uncle's special creams and other cosmetics. She learned everything she could about formulating face creams. She even made suggestions on how to enhance the products. Armed with new formulations, all Estée needed were people to try her products.

IN BUSINESS

Though John Schotz had a laboratory behind Estée's house years earlier, he did not officially open his own business until 1924. That year, he founded New Way Laboratories. Besides making his own products, the chemist also mixed formulas created by others and packaged the products under their brand names. Estée, however, only worked on her uncle's skin care products.

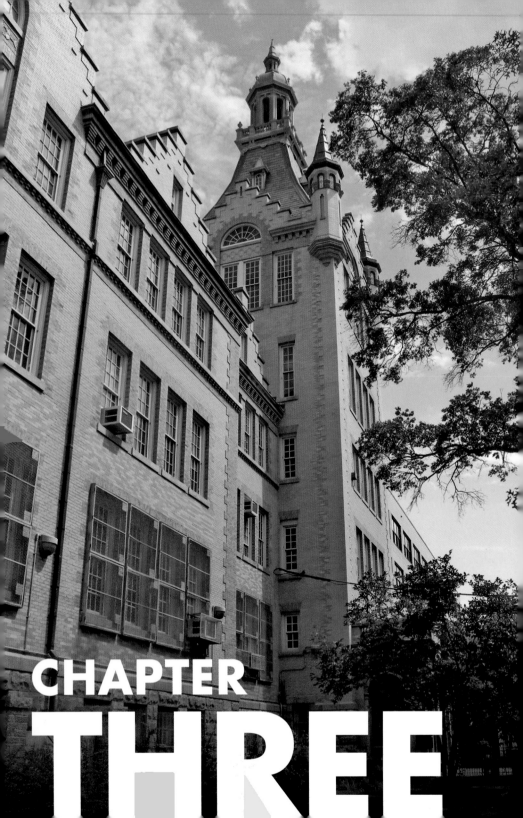

CHAPTER
THREE

A FRESH FACE

Estée attended Newtown High School in Queens, New York. Classmates regularly accompanied her home after school for a facial treatment. Many of her friends were loyal users of the face creams Estée's uncle produced.

"If someone had a slight redness just under her nose that was sure to emerge into a sensitive blemish the next day, she'd come to visit," she would recall years later.[1] In Estée, distressed teenagers found someone their own age who understood their problems and knew how to help. Soon, she had formally named her uncle's face cream Super-Rich All-Purpose Crème, and she packaged it in jars for her friends to take home. The best part about the cream Estée and her uncle produced was that it worked fast. The teenagers who used the cream saw results the next day.

Friends told friends about the cream. Even as a teenager, Estée understood how word-of-mouth advertising worked and just how powerful it could

---

Newtown High School dates back to 1897, and it is still open today.

CREAM OF THE CROP

Face creams made by Lauder's uncle John Schotz were his most popular products, but he created many other products as well. As a chemist, he could not earn a living making and selling only face creams. His other products included mustache wax, drops to ease toothache pain, embalming fluid, paint and varnish remover, muscle-building cream, and a chicken lice killer.

be. More important than the popularity she gained helping her teenage friends was the sense she had found a calling. Estée saw what she was doing as having a meaningful impact on people's lives. She felt sharing her vision of beauty with women and helping them achieve it was honorable, and she wanted to do it for the rest of her life. The skills Estée learned working with her uncle became the root of her beauty empire.

The Mentzer family often spent weekends at Lake Mohegan in upstate New York. Shortly after graduating high school, in 1927, Estée was at the lake with her family. She was sitting on a swing when she heard a friendly voice call out to her. The greeting came from a sharp-looking young man in a golf outfit heading to the nearby course. Estée didn't respond. Her father was strict, and she was certain he would not be pleased if she spoke to a man without a proper introduction. The next weekend, a friend of the

In 1927, Estée and Joseph began a relationship and a partnership that would last more than 50 years.

family formally introduced Estée to the young man. His name was Joseph Lauter. Estée found Joseph to be a shy, gentle man, nowhere near as bold as his original greeting had made him seem.

Joseph Lauter was Estée's first boyfriend. He was six years older than her; Estée was in her late teens and Joseph was in his mid-twenties. However, Estée's parents liked Joseph and gave their approval for the young couple to date. In Joseph, Estée found someone who cherished her and made her feel grown-up. She also found someone who loved Manhattan. He promised her they would live there once they got married. The couple dated for three years and married on January 15, 1930, in New York City. Recalling her wedding day, Estée later said that on that day, Estée Lauder was born.

Into the Salons

In 1937, Estée began using an alternate spelling of her husband's last name, replacing the *T* with a *D*. Lauder spent much of her time in her Manhattan kitchen

AN EQUAL OPPORTUNITY

The cosmetics industry was largely built and run by women. It was one of the few businesses in the early 1900s women could enter as entrepreneurs without being pushed aside by men. Often lacking access to the same business education and financial backing as men, women could launch a cosmetics venture with minimal costs and succeed. Women entrepreneurs developed groundbreaking new beauty products. Many of these products addressed problems shared by both men and women, such as dry skin.

Female entrepreneurs developed innovative sales techniques because mainstream selling avenues were often closed to them. Door-to-door selling, mail orders, stand-alone counters in beauty salons, and home-based sales strategies were all used by women who could not gain shelf space in stores controlled by men. Women such as Estée Lauder, Elizabeth Arden, Helena Rubinstein, Madame Walker, and Annie Turnbo were entrepreneurs who made their fortunes in cosmetics.

Cosmetics businesses opened up many opportunities for women to find jobs in the beauty industry. Women entered the cosmetics business in various capacities—from product development to management to advertising to public relations.

formulating new products. The beauty mogul was always looking for ways to make her face creams work better and please the senses with exotic fragrances. She was happiest mixing new batches of face cream. With each new batch, she hoped to discover something magical—a cream that gave women a look they never thought possible. She learned early in her career that "to sell a cream, you sold a dream."[2]

The couple had their first child, Leonard, on March 19, 1933. When her son was very young, Lauder would take walks with him down to the Cherry Lane Theater, not far from their apartment. She sometimes convinced show producers to give her small parts in their plays. However, she did not get the same thrill from acting as she did from making women fit her vision of beauty. Once again, she turned her attention to the jars of magic she brewed up at home.

As a young mother, Lauder looked forward to getting her hair done at a beauty salon called House of

SPEAKING OF COSMETICS

Lauder enlarged her customer base by giving beauty talks at charity events. She made her talks fun and entertaining and even applied her makeup on willing members of the audience. At the events, she gave away samples of her products. Many women tried them, liked them, and became paying customers.

Ash Blondes. She persuaded many of the young mothers she met at the salon to stop by her apartment for beauty lessons. One day the owner of the salon, Florence Morris, asked Lauder how she made her skin look so fresh. The next time Lauder came to the salon, she brought a bag full of her skin care treatments. The bag contained Cleansing Oil, Crème Pack, Super-Rich All-Purpose Crème, a light skin lotion, face powder, and lipstick.

Florence Morris was busy when Lauder arrived and asked her to leave the products at the salon. But Lauder was not about to leave without giving the salon owner a full demonstration. She assured Morris she could show her the full line of products in just five minutes. Working her magic, Lauder treated the woman's face and completed the demonstration in the promised five minutes. When she was done, Morris made Lauder a job

Lipstick became one of Lauder's signature products.

offer. She wanted Lauder to sell cosmetics at another of her New York City beauty salons.

Lauder would pay rent for her space at the salon, but she could keep whatever money she made from the products she sold. She would have her own counter space and sell her own products. Estée Lauder was in business.

CHAPTER
FOUR

LIFE LESSONS

Lauder was determined to turn her counter at the beauty salon into her big business break. She was an excellent saleswoman, providing her customers with products she absolutely believed in. She lavished customers with her undivided attention; what was important to them was important to her. The women loved how Lauder treated them.

Her excellent memory, which she hoped at one time to use in becoming a great actress, was an important asset in sales. She remembered each of her customers and asked about their lives whenever she saw them. It made her sales approach warm and personal. If one of her customers was pregnant, Lauder always made sure she knew when the baby was due to be born. After, she would send a basket of her products to the new mom. The dedicated entrepreneur let no detail slip by her.

Lauder sold her products by day and made her products at home at night. "I didn't need bread to eat,

Throughout her career, Lauder loved to give hands-on demonstrations of her products to customers.

but I worked as though I did . . . from pure love of the venture," she remembered.[1]

Her Own Best Saleswoman

In her early entrepreneurial days, Lauder stopped women on the street, walking down halls, or in elevators. She complimented them on some aspect of their appearance and then steered the conversation

SELLING IN HARD TIMES

From her home, in beauty salons, and at resorts, Lauder sold her cosmetics in good times and bad. She sold during the 1930s, a very difficult time for the nation. The country was going through the Great Depression, a time of high unemployment and numerous bank failures. But Lauder discovered the economic downturn did not prevent women from buying cosmetics products—especially if the products worked well. She believed people would always spend money on a good product. World War II (1939–1945) broke out on the heels of the Great Depression. The United States was at war from 1941 to 1945. Cosmetics remained popular. Even Rosie the Riveter, the face of the female defense worker, was shown wearing lipstick. With men going to war and women replacing them in the workplace, more women were buying makeup. As they ventured into the worlds of business and industry, some men criticized them, saying that by taking men's jobs they lost their femininity. Many women used makeup to maintain a feminine appearance and fight this criticism.

By the war's end, Lauder's products were selling better than ever before. The beauty business as a whole was booming. In 1946, the New York Times ran an article calling cosmetics a billion-dollar business, and Lauder was right in the middle of it.

toward skin care. Lauder was so knowledgeable about skin issues she could tell what type of problems a person had at a glance. And she usually had the solution.

On weekends, Lauder traveled to resorts in New York's Catskill Mountains or on Long Island. She gave entertaining beauty talks that women rushed to hear. She performed makeovers on each of the women who attended her talks, and few left without buying her products. Many became regular customers. Whenever she had a spare minute, Lauder would go poolside, giving out beauty tips and doing makeovers for women lounging in the sun. As a result, she sold even more products.

Lauder was so confident about the products she was selling she cast aside conventional sales techniques and

LIFELONG CATALYST

One day, while Lauder was working at Florence Morris's beauty salon, she complimented a woman on her blouse. Lauder said the blouse was elegant and asked the woman where she had bought it. The woman said, "What difference could it possibly make? You could never afford it."[2] Lauder was mortified and vowed to never let anyone speak to her like that again. She later told the story many times, even beginning her autobiography with it. She called it a "catalyst" for her success: "Maybe I wouldn't have become Estée Lauder if it hadn't been for her."[3]

pioneered an entirely new way of selling products. Rather than putting a jar of her product in a woman's hand and extolling its virtues, she would open the jar and lovingly apply the product, showing the potential customer how to use it. "Touch your customer, and you're halfway there," she said in an interview.[4] Lauder wanted to pass her passion for her product line on to her customers. "I love to touch the creams, smell them, look at them, carry them with me. A person has to love her harvest if she's to expect others to love it," she contended.[5] Even if a woman did not buy her products, the confident entrepreneur would give her a free sample anyway, certain that once the woman used the product, she would return to buy a full-sized jar.

Lauder had a daily goal. She wanted to make every customer feel as if she was the only woman receiving her attention that day. Every face and every woman were

Word of mouth among her customers helped to popularize Lauder's products even when she could not afford expensive advertisements.

important to her. Lauder wanted every woman who came to see her to leave feeling good about herself, to have a positive attitude about the experience, and to tell another woman about it. That last point was critical to Lauder's growing business, especially since she had no money for advertising. She called it her "Tell-a-Woman Campaign," and was convinced that word of mouth would make her business a success. It worked. Soon, women were seeking out Lauder's products, determined to buy them before even meeting her. Some women would only go to beauty salons where Estée Lauder products were being sold. They heard positive reviews from other women who used the products, looked good, and were happy with the service they received.

WORD OF MOUTH

"Tell-a-Woman," the word-of-mouth advertising campaign Lauder used in the start-up days of her cosmetics business, was very successful. Though her business was located in New York City, she received orders from women who lived as far away as Philadelphia, Long Island, Westchester County in upstate New York, and parts of Connecticut.

Expansion and Tension

Lauder began hearing from other beauty salons that wanted to sell her products. She could not travel to so many salons at once, so she needed to hire saleswomen. Lauder ran employment notices in newspapers and held interviews. She was very particular about her saleswomen. They had to know every aspect of the products, including how to apply them properly. They had to be warm, caring, and not overly aggressive.

Lauder did not want her saleswomen to push products on people. She believed it would drive customers away. Lauder once had 20 women apply for sales positions, only finding one who met her exacting standards. Soon she had saleswomen working at several locations, but she still visited them all as often as she could. She wanted to make sure each sale was being handled properly. Her only regret was she could not always be present at every counter to make every sale.

Lauder's enormous drive to succeed, however, was causing problems at home. Her husband, Joseph, did not share his wife's vision of establishing a huge beauty empire. To make things worse, they were both working hard, yet she was making progress faster than he was. In the 1930s and 1940s, women were rarely the more financially successful partner, and Joseph had trouble adjusting to the situation. Lauder wrote in her autobiography that when her husband wanted to talk, she was off in another world. This put tremendous stress on the marriage. The couple divorced on April 11, 1939, barely nine years after getting married. Lauder would later say she knew instantly the divorce was a mistake.

Following the breakup of her marriage, Lauder divided her time between her home in New York City and Florida, where her mother lived. While in Florida, she began selling her products in local beauty salons. She dated occasionally, but Lauder missed her former husband. "I kept needing to tell Joe something funny

MUMPS: A LOVE STORY

A case of the mumps got the Lauders back together. Though they had divorced, the couple still saw each other a great deal because of the love they shared for their son, Leonard. One day, the boy came down with a high fever. It was the onset of the mumps, and Lauder called her ex-husband right away. He rushed to her side. The two nursed Leonard back to health and realized they should be together. They remarried shortly thereafter.

that had happened. . . . In a sea of new experiences and people, I was lonely. I missed the gentle solidness of the darling man I'd married in the first place," Lauder said.[7]

The couple remarried on December 7, 1942. Lauder vowed to better balance her work and home lives. Joseph, coming around to supporting her career, agreed to enter her business as an equal partner. Though their life would be built around their business, the couple still wanted to expand their family. Ronald, the couple's second son, was born on February 26, 1944. The new baby did little to temper Lauder's ambitions. Soon after Ronald's birth, she was hard at work implementing the next phase of her business plan.

Ronald Lauder would stay close with his mother for the rest of her life.

CHAPTER
FIVE

EXPANDING
THE BRAND

Lauder was more confident than ever her business would reap the financial rewards she always thought possible. Her husband's involvement in the enterprise strengthened her resolve. The couple was so sure the venture would succeed they invested all their savings to rent space in Manhattan to open a small factory. The building's owner wanted six months' rent up front—a big commitment for the Lauders to make at the time. But the business was getting too big for Lauder to mix and package her products at home.

The building was formerly a restaurant, which worked well for the Lauders. The couple used the kitchen equipment to formulate their products. They also invested some of their savings in new bottles and packaging. Estée felt the products should have exciting-looking bottles and their own color scheme. The Estée Lauder line had to stand out on store shelves so

After reuniting, Lauder and her husband set out to succeed in the difficult cosmetics business.

customers could spot it right away, she reasoned. She was convinced the extra investment would pay off in the long run.

The investment went against the advice of both their accountant and their lawyer. The two professionals felt the Lauders were making a big mistake by going into the cosmetics business full time. They took the Lauders out to dinner, trying to persuade them to halt the business venture. "The mortality rate in the cosmetics industry is high, and you'll rue the day you invested your savings and your time in this impossible business," Estée recalled the men saying.[1] She would hear none of it. Neither would her husband. The Estée Lauder Company was formally established in 1946.

A Gift with Every Purchase

Around the same time, Lauder started a practice that set a standard in the cosmetics industry. She had reached the point where many people were regular customers. Meanwhile, she was busy trying to develop new products to add to her line. As she did, she would include a sample of her latest product with every sale she made, hoping to get people to try the new product. It did not take long for her to see that everybody loved getting the free gift, and many went on to purchase the new product. People who received the gifts felt their purchase was appreciated. It helped keep regular customers loyal to the brand and bring in new customers.

The division of labor between the Lauders was clear. Joseph ran the factory, while Estée sold the products. In the late 1940s, Lauder traveled the nation, visiting stores of all types and sizes, establishing cosmetics counters with her products, and giving demonstrations. She was determined to get her products in the finest department stores. These included Bonwit Teller, Macy's, Neiman Marcus, and her ultimate goal—Saks Fifth Avenue in Manhattan.

She mastered the technique of the three-minute makeover. Using cosmetics products, she could make women look the way they wanted in just three minutes.

WOMAN'S INTUITION

Estée Lauder's free-gift promotion was a simple yet ingenious advertising strategy. It took no elaborate planning, but it proved extremely effective. The strategy was based purely on Lauder's strong belief in the quality of her products. Lauder was confident that when a woman got a free sample of her cosmetics, she would return to purchase more of it. Soon, many women made purchases just to get the free gift—typically a sample of Lauder's latest product.

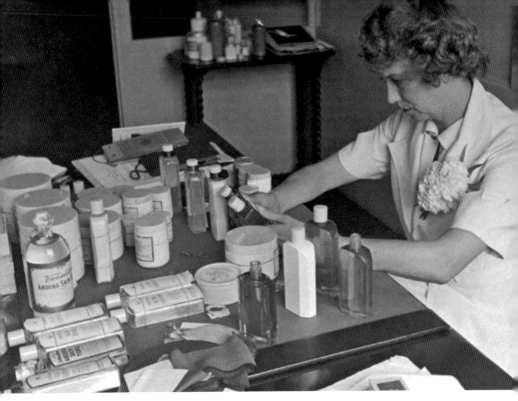

Lauder faced fierce competition from established giants in the beauty business, such as Elizabeth Arden.

Every woman at the demonstrations who wanted a makeover got one. Lauder and her hired assistants could do hundreds in a day. She never seemed to tire. Her persistence soon proved necessary.

There was enormous competition in the 1940s and 1950s to place products in high-end department stores such as Bonwit Teller and Saks Fifth Avenue. This was especially true of cosmetics products. Elizabeth Arden, Helena Rubinstein, Dorothy Gray, and Revlon were all big brand names in the beauty business. They were all competing for customers, and department stores that catered to the upper class were not looking to offer any new product lines. Yet Lauder was not discouraged.

High-end department stores sold the most elegant fashions of the day. As far as Lauder was concerned, her product line complemented and completed these outfits. She felt her products belonged in the stores. When she was not on the road selling her products, Lauder was in the offices of department store buyers. These workers decided what products would end up on the shelves of their stores. Lauder argued her product line would succeed.

TO HER CREDIT

Before the days of ubiquitous universal credit cards, such as MasterCard and Visa, which became widely available in the 1960s, high-end department stores offered customers store charge accounts. Customers could purchase goods on credit and then pay a single bill each month. Lauder believed customers tended to buy more if they could charge their purchases. That was one of the reasons she coveted counter space in these fashionable department stores.

Dogged Determination

No matter how many times department store managers turned down Lauder's requests for counter space, she always returned. "Success depends on daring to act on dreams," she said.[2] She refused to be put off and later joked her efforts came close to outright nagging. Yet she had research to back up her claims. Lauder studied the products these high-end retailers carried and knew her product line ranked with the best cosmetics the stores had to offer. The determined entrepreneur contended her loyal customers were just the type of shoppers these stores wanted. She reasoned her customer base was satisfied and growing. What's more, her customers were willing to spend money on cosmetics.

Finally, in late 1947, Bonwit Teller gave counter space to the Estée Lauder Company. Lauder was ready to prove the store right. Though she had hired saleswomen, Lauder herself often worked behind the counter at Bonwit Teller. Saturday was a big shopping day at the department store, and she spent the whole day there every week.

Lauder also continued pursuing Saks Fifth Avenue. Every Wednesday and Friday, Saks's buyers met with representatives from different companies who wanted to sell products at the prestigious store. Lauder attended these meetings for weeks. Finally, at a meeting in 1948, Bob Fiske, the cosmetics buyer for the store, told her he simply did not see a demand for her products among Saks customers. He told her if she could prove there was demand for her line, her cosmetics would be considered for the store. It was all Lauder needed to hear. Soon

IN THE MAIL

By 1950, Lauder was making enough money from her cosmetics to establish an advertising budget of more than $50,000 per year. She got several recommendations for notable advertising firms to handle the account, but none would take on her company as a client. The firms felt her budget was too small to launch a successful, ongoing campaign. But Lauder always had a backup plan. She decided to use the money to print a variety of attractive flyers. She then worked out an arrangement with Saks. The store would include the flyers when mailing out its monthly charge account bills to customers. The flyers advertised Lauder's latest products and offered a free gift to customers who visited the Estée Lauder counter at Saks.

The Saks mailing list was a very powerful tool for Lauder. She did a tremendous amount of direct mailing using the list, advertising directly to the people who were interested in her products. Saks customers liked the flyers and loved the free gifts. They often bought products when they visited the Estée Lauder counter, especially if Lauder herself was there to give advice or demonstrations.

Landing products in Saks Fifth Avenue gave the Estée Lauder Company a big boost.

after, she scheduled a cosmetics demonstration and luncheon at the Waldorf-Astoria Hotel, just a few blocks away from Saks.

The demonstration at the Waldorf drew a large crowd of women. Lauder gave each one a free lipstick. Many tried and liked it immediately. They asked where they could buy more. Lauder told them to ask for the lipstick at Saks Fifth Avenue. The women left the luncheon and formed a long line at Saks.

Fiske contacted Lauder later that day and made arrangements to carry her line of products. She later described getting into Saks as one of the most exciting moments of her life. Once Lauder had the breakthrough at Saks, she shifted her focus away from beauty salons and concentrated her full attention on department store sales. To let her customers know she was at Saks, she sent them gold-lettered cards on white paper announcing her new location. Naturally, she invited everyone to stop by and get a free gift.

THE BIGGER PICTURE

When Lauder went to a department store to sell, she would not spend all her time at the cosmetics counter. She also visited the hat, shoe, and dress departments, giving out product samples to salespeople along the way. If they liked her products, Lauder reasoned, they might send their customers to her counter. She also gave samples to saleswomen working at other cosmetics counters, thinking if they did not have the shade of lipstick a customer wanted, the saleswomen would refer their customers to the Estée Lauder counter.

CHAPTER
SIX

GAINING MORE GROUND

The success at Saks spurred Lauder on. She now set her sights on the luxury department store Neiman Marcus, headquartered in Dallas, Texas. Lauder hated flying, but she felt getting into Neiman Marcus was worth it. In the winter of 1950, she traveled to Dallas. She went to the store every day until the store president, Stanley Marcus, agreed to meet with her late one afternoon. Lauder wasted no time with her sales pitch: "I'm Estée Lauder and I have the most wonderful beauty products in the world and they must be in your store."[1]

The store already carried several cosmetics lines, including Elizabeth Arden's, but Lauder got her foot in the door and was not going to take it out. She insisted Neiman Marcus customers needed her products right away. Marcus had never met anyone so persistent. That impressed him, and he asked Lauder how much space she thought she would need in the store. She told him

Lauder's confidence and persistence carried her into new markets, expanding the reach of her brand dramatically.

she could make her counter work with just four or five feet (1.2 or 1.5 m). Marcus thought for a while. "When can you have your merchandise here?" he later remembered saying to her. He later recalled, "Well, by God, she had it all with her. She had brought a big bag filled with merchandise, and the very next day she set it

ATTENTION TO EVERY DETAIL

For Lauder, every little detail mattered when it came to selling cosmetics. At first, she packaged her products in white jars with black caps. But she soon decided those jars were ordinary, uninspiring, and medicinal looking. She wanted her jars to look exciting, enticing, and elegant, so she sought to design jars with an aura of mystery and beauty. She conducted research to find a color that would not clash with her customers' bathroom furnishings. She obtained samples of different jars in various shapes, sizes, and colors, and carried the samples in her purse.

Whenever she visited people's homes or ate at exclusive restaurants, she excused herself so she could go to the bathroom. There, she would take out the bottles from her purse and see how they looked in the room. Lauder analyzed how each bottle complemented or clashed with the various wallpapers, fixtures, and tiles.

Finally, she decided on an array of unusually shaped jars, each holding a different product. The color of the jars would be uniform, a mix of blue and green Lauder called "a fragile, pale turquoise that was memorable."[2] Within the company, the color later became known as "Estée blue."

up and she was in business at Neiman Marcus. . . . It was easier to say yes to Estée than to say no."[3]

Ground Rules

Determined to open as many department store counters as she could, Lauder established some ground rules for herself. She would open each of the new counters herself and spend a week at each store. She made sure each display was attractive and inviting. And at each counter, she offered free gifts with every purchase and free makeovers to anyone who wanted one.

Lauder sought a special kind of saleswoman. She wanted people who knew how to sell but who also cared about the products. Each prospective saleswoman had to use the products herself. She had to be happy selling the products. Lauder wanted elegant, refined saleswomen behind her counter.

MYSTERY SHOPPERS

Lauder felt it was extremely important for her customers to receive top-notch service. She decided to hire mystery shoppers to make sure her counters were being run properly. These shoppers would make unannounced visits to department stores where Lauder's products were sold, observe sales, and report back to the company. If there was a problem, Lauder would go out and correct it herself, no matter where the store was located.

MAKING THE BEST OF IT

When Lauder made an appearance at Himelhoch's Department Store in Detroit, Michigan, she found the store had only two shades of her lipstick in stock: deep red and pale coral. A long line of women had gathered to meet her and see her demonstrate the full product line. Lauder improvised. She showed the women how to combine deep red and pale coral lipstick to achieve a stylish look. She advised they use the darker color over the lighter one in the evening and the lighter color over the darker one in the daytime. Within hours, the store sold out of both shades.

Despite her hectic schedule, Lauder was always thinking of new products she could add to her line. One of those products was her combination bath oil and fragrance, Youth Dew. Perfume production worldwide had been slowed by World War II. Many of the perfume factories were used to produce medical products for the war effort. Perfume factories, especially in Europe, were slow to restart fragrance production after the war. In 1953, Lauder felt her new fragrance would find a receptive audience. At first, she offered Youth Dew as the free gift with every purchase. Customers loved the samples and demanded the product in larger quantities. Youth Dew sales in the United States soared throughout the 1950s. It made the Estée Lauder Company the number three line behind beauty industry stalwarts Helena Rubinstein

Helena Rubinstein had been selling cosmetics to
women since before Lauder was born.

and Elizabeth Arden. The explosive introduction of Youth Dew into the beauty business made Rubinstein and Arden take note. They both began viewing Lauder as serious competition.

International Ambitions

Though Youth Dew was taking the United States by storm, Estée Lauder had bigger plans for her fragrance. She envisioned Youth Dew being sold in Europe as well. In 1958, her son Leonard joined the company, taking on some of the business burden and giving Lauder time to push Youth Dew overseas. Leonard was fresh out of the US Navy when he joined the family business. He had graduated from the Wharton School of Business at the University of Pennsylvania before enlisting and was now ready to put his business skills to use. His parents always kept him updated on big business decisions in the hope he would want to make the

BORN INTO THE BUSINESS

In the early days of Lauder's business, her son Leonard would help his father fill bottles at the couple's small New York City factory. He also delivered products by bicycle to some of Lauder's clients. Leonard was in high school, but he learned about all the hard work that went into making a business successful.

Elaborate fashion shows are often held at the prestigious Galeries Lafayette in Paris.

Estée Lauder Company his life's work. One of Lauder's goals was to keep her business in the family.

By early 1960, she was ready to start her European sales pitch for Youth Dew. She had a plan similar to the one she used to establish counter space in upscale US department stores. Lauder set out with product in hand to meet with buyers at European department stores, such as Galeries Lafayette in Paris, France. She was convinced that Youth Dew deserved counter space in Galeries Lafayette even though the store was located in a country synonymous with fragrances, where perfumes were created and revered. Buyers at Galeries

Estée Lauder's company continued pursuing international markets, eventually partnering with Chinese authorities to open a research facility in China.

Lafayette could not imagine French women purchasing an American-made perfume. Try as she might, Lauder was not having any luck persuading them to try her fragrance.

Lauder became friendly with some of the saleswomen at the French department store. She stopped to talk to one of them while in the store one day. The subject turned to perfume, and Lauder took a bottle of Youth Dew out of her purse. While showing the French woman the perfume that was turning heads in

America, she spilled some on the floor. It did not take long for the fragrance to start wafting through the store. Shoppers demanded to know more about the scent. The saleswomen admitted it came from a bottle of American perfume. In a matter of weeks, Youth Dew was on the shelves of the most elegant department store in France. It began selling throughout Europe, and then crossed the US border north to Canada. Estée Lauder was now an international brand.

SKIN DEEP

Lauder always realized skin problems were not an issue faced only by women. Men faced many of the same problems. She often told a story about a Saint Louis, Missouri, woman whose adolescent son had terrible skin problems. Her son, the woman told Lauder, would not use any of that "woman's stuff" on his face, referring to the products women used to keep their skin clear. Knowing her Crème Pack worked equally well on males and females, Lauder poured some into a plain jar. She gave it to the woman for her son to use. He tried it, and his problems were solved.

CHAPTER
SEVEN

INNOVATIONS

The beauty business was facing major changes in the 1960s, just as Estée Lauder was continuing her rise as a major player in the industry. Revenues from Youth Dew enabled her to expand her line of cosmetics and venture boldly into new areas.

In 1960, the company introduced one of its most expensive products ever. Re-Nutriv was Lauder's new luxury face cream. Unlike her other creams, which carried a price tag most everyone could afford, Re-Nutriv sold for the lofty price of $115 per pound (0.45 kg). The cream offered women a new formula using rare ingredients. It came out in an era when European companies were making claims about miraculous face creams that would remove wrinkles and give skin a more youthful appearance.

At the same time, the Food and Drug Administration was carefully checking claims made by cosmetics companies in the United States. Nevertheless, all the big beauty companies were anxious to take advantage

In the 1960s, Lauder introduced innovative products and marketing strategies to the world of cosmetics.

of this latest skin care craze. Revlon released Ultima, a cream the company claimed went deep into living cells, and Helena Rubinstein marketed Bio-Facial Treatment, which supposedly penetrated the skin's pores. Advertising for these products linked them to the latest laboratory discoveries.

A Memorable Ad

Lauder promoted Re-Nutriv differently than her other products. She wanted the product's name, which sounded somewhat scientific, to conjure up

JUST FOR MEN

In the 1960s, men rarely bought their own high-end colognes. They purchased shaving cream and aftershave in local drugstores, but they usually received upscale fragrances as gifts. Men's cologne choices were paltry. Lauder aimed to convince men to use their own scents.

To achieve this, she launched the Aramis line of cosmetics in 1965. The line included upscale soap, aftershave, cologne, and shaving lotion. Aramis was not successful at first, but Lauder refused to give up on it. Slowly and steadily she built up the line, backing it with advertising dollars. Eventually, Aramis found its niche and started selling well in the 1970s.

The product line saw a dramatic increase in sales in 1981 thanks to a successful television ad campaign. The commercials featured Ted Danson, the actor who would go on to star in the hit sitcom *Cheers*. The commercials showed an attractive woman doing a double take after a suave Danson, wearing Aramis, passes by during a chance meeting.

in people's minds the notion it was grounded in science. Meanwhile, she took out a full-page advertisement in the popular magazine *Harper's Bazaar*—the first full-page ad the company had ever placed. The ad's headline got right to the point, asking the question, "What Makes a Cream Worth $115.00?" The ad then listed the extraordinary and expensive ingredients that went into Re-Nutriv, including turtle oil, silicone, and royal jelly from bees. The ads also played on Lauder's reputation in the industry: "But above all the rare perception of a woman like Estée Lauder who knows almost better then anyone how to keep you looking younger, fresher, lovelier than you ever dreamed possible," the ad copy stated.[1]

Word spread quickly that Re-Nutriv left customers' skin looking radiant and feeling revitalized. Lauder

CHANGING LANDSCAPE

The deaths of Helena Rubinstein in 1965 at age 94 and Elizabeth Arden in 1966 at age 81 changed the landscape of the beauty industry. Both companies were sold and no longer run by family members of the original founders. Lauder's company remained independent, and she became the reigning queen of the beauty industry. While the other companies shifted their sales strategies, Lauder kept her focus squarely on innovation and the upper-class market. With her fellow entrepreneurs gone, the media looked to Lauder for commentary on the latest trends in cosmetics.

Advertising and in-person demonstrations helped
Lauder sell the expensive Re-Nutriv products.

traveled to department stores across the country and
once again sold the product herself. Re-Nutriv's price
and Lauder's hands-on promotion spurred the news
media to write about the new, exotic-sounding face
cream, bringing the product additional attention. An
air of secrecy and exclusivity surrounded the product.
Its formula was said to be known only to the Lauder
family and kept in a vault to which only they had access.
No specific medical claims were made in connection
with the product. It was simply said to contain the best
and most expensive ingredients. Re-Nutriv, though
expensive, found a customer base. It became another

star in Lauder's growing galaxy of successful products. Re-Nutriv lent additional support to one of Lauder's theories—people would spend money on a product that worked.

The Lauder Woman

In 1962, Lauder devised another innovation in the beauty industry—the Lauder woman. The concept was ingenious: to use the same model in all of the company's advertisements to project a singular image of the products and the company. Other cosmetics companies used a variety of models to advertise their products in ads that seemed to blend together. None of them stood out.

Nobody knew at a glance which model represented which company. Instant recognition was the goal of introducing the Lauder woman. People looked at an Estée Lauder ad and knew instantly which company's

PRIVATE STOCK

Lauder developed one fragrance she kept for herself. Women who visited her often asked the name of the perfume she was wearing. She would simply say it came from her private collection. At times, she would share it with them. Word spread about the secret scent until finally the buyer from Saks Fifth Avenue called, saying, "That private collection of yours? We must have it, Mrs. Lauder."[2] Lauder marketed the scent as an Estée Lauder exclusive, concluding that women want what is not available to everybody else.

WOMEN OF COLOR

For many years, all of the women hired as Lauder women to represent the company were exclusively white. At the time, Lauder's products were created for and sold nearly exclusively to upper-class white women. Eventually, the company began to manufacture and market different shades of their products to cater to a wider and more diverse base of customers. Finally, in 2003, model Liya Kebede became the first African-American woman to become a Lauder woman.

products were being advertised before even reading the ad's words. Lauder believed the recognition factor added to the value of the advertisement.

The first Lauder woman was discovered by accident, when Leonard Lauder saw a picture photographer Victor Skrebneski sent to the company. Skrebneski was just becoming a notable fashion photographer. His black-and-white photo depicted Chicago model Phyllis Connor as a self-assured, motivated, successful woman. Leonard took the photo to Estée. She liked it but wanted Skrebneski to make the image sharper. She pushed the photographer to hone his technique and demanded the same excellence in the photos that she required in the production of her cosmetics.

The ads appeared in fashionable magazines, such as *Vogue*, *Harper's Bazaar*, *Town & Country*, and *The New Yorker*. They appeared in black and white because

Lauder's company could not afford the more expensive color ads. Still, the ads were striking. The model, her designer clothes, and the upscale furnishings in the background all contributed to the power of the ads. The overall image the ads conveyed was based on the lifestyle Lauder had always imagined for herself. Copywriter June Leaman, who had worked for the renowned department store Bergdorf Goodman before coming to the Estée Lauder Company, wrote the wording for the ads. Leaman helped develop the mystique of the Lauder woman with her ad copy: "She has the confident look of a woman with the world in the palm of her hand. Seeing her in the Estée Lauder world, you somehow know that her closets are impeccable, her children well-behaved, her husband devoted and her guests pampered."[3]

The advertisements became an important part of the company's image. In later years, supermodel Karen Graham became the Lauder woman. Graham was so closely associated with the company many people thought she was Estée Lauder herself. Other models followed in the role of the Lauder woman, including Elizabeth Hurley, Willow Bay, and Carolyn Murphy.

Actress and Lauder woman Elizabeth Hurley appeared in ads for many of the company's products, including Perfectionist Wrinkle Lifting Serum in 2008.

The Next New Thing

Lauder never stopped thinking about the next big product or trend in cosmetics. Like Youth Dew, new products or trends had to fill a void in the beauty industry. This was the only way to create the earth-shattering impact that makes one cosmetics company stand out from the rest. Lauder felt she had an idea that would do just that, but it involved some risk. "Leonard said it many times: if there was a brand-new concept that could compete with Estée Lauder, he wanted Estée Lauder to introduce it," the beauty mogul recalled.[4]

Estée talked to Leonard about her idea, which was to developing a line of hypoallergenic cosmetics. These products would be for the millions of women who could not wear many of the makeup products on the market because of allergies. Existing products were generally drab, unimaginative, and medicinal in look and scent. They did not sit on the counter with the rest of the cosmetics. There was nothing glamorous or exciting about them. Big cosmetics companies were not willing to fully commit to hypoallergenics. Charles Revson, the head of Revlon, felt the field was a "drag."[5] To Lauder, this was an opening to develop a whole new line of hypoallergenic cosmetics that would be exhilarating— and profitable. In 1968, the Clinique line of products was born.

CLINIQUE

CLINIQUE
superfit makeup
oil-free, long-wear

CLINIQUE
perfectly real
makeup

CLINIQUE
superbalanced
makeup

CHAPTER
EIGHT

NEW VENTURES

Lauder decided to launch Clinique as a separate brand. Anything released under the Clinique brand would be 100 percent allergy tested and fragrance-free. Her interest in this area came from reading about the work of Dr. Norman Orentreich in 1967. Dr. Orentreich ran a skin clinic in New York. He had an excellent reputation for the research he had done into sensitive skin in both men and women. He also treated many patients who suffered skin irritations and had successfully cured them.

Around the same time, *Vogue* magazine was running a series of articles about great skin. The magazine consulted a well-known dermatologist for the story. As it turned out, the dermatologist was Orentreich. Estée and Leonard were looking for a skin expert to formulate the Clinique line, so they contacted Orentreich and the three met. It was the first time Estée brought in a medical doctor as a consultant. The collaboration went well; Orentreich agreed to work with the Lauder

Lauder would sell the Clinique brand as having allergy-free, science-based formulas.

BRAND NEW

To avoid confusion in the marketplace, Lauder thought it best to make Clinique a separate brand. She was developing a totally new product and wanted customers to realize Clinique was different from any cosmetic they had ever tried before. She also felt the product line had a better chance to grow and become successful under its own brand name. One thing remained the same: there was a free gift with every purchase.

chemists to develop the Clinique line.

Lauder decided to launch a full Clinique product line rather than a single product. She wanted women who needed hypoallergenic cosmetics to have choices about the products they used. It was rare for a cosmetics company to roll out an entire product line all at once. Usually, one product was launched at a time. If it proved successful, the money made from that product was used to build a line around it. Clinique was different. Lauder felt customers had to see how all the products worked together to understand the full breadth of the line. At the time of the launch in September 1968, the line consisted of a whopping 117 products.

Carol Phillips, formerly the managing editor of *Vogue* magazine, was hired as Clinique's president. She established the entire brand in the span of eight months. Lauder's younger son, Ronald, became executive vice president of Clinique Laboratories.

A Hush-Hush Venture

There was great secrecy surrounding the creation of the hypoallergenic line because of the competitive nature of the cosmetics business. No other company seemed to have an interest in hypoallergenic products. Still, Lauder believed if they knew she was working on such products, they might attempt to create their own line and beat her to the market. Only a few people within the company knew about Clinique. It was developed under the code name *Mrs. Lauder*. If anyone wanted to write a memo or discuss the development of the hypoallergenic product

SPIES

Formulas for cosmetics have always been closely guarded industry secrets. Only members of the Lauder family knew the full, exact formula for Estée Lauder products. Lauder was convinced her fierce rival, Charles Revson of Revlon, was spying on her company. After earlier scoffing at the concept of hypoallergenic cosmetics, Revlon released a line to compete with Clinique. When Estée Lauder unveiled Aramis for men in 1965, Revlon produced Braggi for men in 1966. Revlon began offering free gifts with purchases, mimicking Lauder's promotion. At the Estée Lauder offices, employees would say, "50 percent of Revlon's R&D [research and development] was done here."[1]

Revson's actions angered Lauder, leading to a feud between the two cosmetics companies. After Revson's death in 1975, Lauder admitted his cloak-and-dagger techniques kept her on her toes. Revson's biographer, Andrew Tobias, wrote about Lauder: "She was the one competitor he [Revson] set out to beat but couldn't."[2]

line, it was referred to by that name. Each product in the line had its own code name as well.

Clinique was not an instant success. Lauder invested millions of dollars to produce and market the line. Carol Phillips, Ronald Lauder, and Leonard Lauder believed in the line and felt the investment would eventually pay off.

Clinique saleswomen, called consultants, were rigorously trained in all aspects of the new product line and the skin problems it addressed. They wore white lab coats to project a clinical look. The consultants were very careful about the products they sold. The company instructed them to ask questions about a customer's complexion history. If, after hearing the answers to the questions, the consultant felt Clinique was the wrong product for the customer, the consultant would not sell her the product. "If a customer requested something that would be wrong for her, we wouldn't sell it. That is the truth," Lauder later said.[3]

The new brand established an industry standard in managerial patience. The Lauders knew Clinique had all the elements needed to succeed. Women who tried the products appreciated the science behind them. It was just a matter of getting enough women to discover it. Clinique lost $3 million before it began making money

In-store demonstrations were key to Clinique's success as a brand.

in 1975. By 1978, the brand was bringing in $80 million a year, nearly 30 percent of the Estée Lauder Company's revenues. In 1981, *Forbes* magazine called Clinique the "walkaway leader" in its field. The magazine reported, "The Lauders spent the money, took the losses for a while and nourished the business."[4]

Lauder extolled the virtues of a family-owned business, noting other types of businesses might not have given Clinique the time it needed to develop. A publicly owned company controlled by stockholders, Lauder contended, would have given up on the venture at the first sign of losses. Revenues from Clinique continued to increase each year. No hypoallergenic line on the market could compete.

The Social Scene

In 1972, Leonard became president of the Estée Lauder Company. Estée, who had held the title of president, became chairman of the board. With both sons working for her company, just as she had hoped, Estée turned her attention to another passion—the social scene. She now had time to throw all the lavish parties she wanted at her homes in Manhattan and Long Island, New York; Palm Beach, Florida; London, England; and the French Riviera, France. She had the chance to live the social life she always dreamed about and become friendly with the most famous people in the world.

Lauder's parties were a prestigious place for people to be seen in the 1970s. Just like her cosmetics lines, her parties

COMFORTS OF HOME

Lauder was as creative in decorating her many homes as she was in developing her product line. Each of her homes had a theme. For instance, her home on the French Riviera had an extraordinary garden modeled after the gardens depicted in the work of impressionist artist Claude Monet. Her home in London featured antique British furniture.

had to be perfect. She had the finest linens, food, music, and service. Everything was color coordinated. There was one waiter for every two people, and all of the waiters wore white gloves. Formal attire was required, champagne flowed, and only elite members of society were invited.

Lauder believed her parties and the notoriety that came from hosting them were all good for business. She thought her appearances on the pages of newspapers drew customers and added to the cachet of the Estée

Lauder brand. She worked hard to improve her social standing, always looking for ways to meet people who could positively impact her business.

One of the couples Lauder most wanted to befriend was the Duke and Duchess of Windsor. She came close to meeting the royal couple on several occasions but kept missing them. Both she and the couple had homes in Palm Beach. Lauder knew that, like herself, the Duchess was uncomfortable flying and usually took the train

Lauder befriended many high-profile people, including Raisa Gorbachev, wife of the president of the Soviet Union.

between New York and Florida. Lauder found out when the Duke and Duchess were leaving Palm Beach and the location of their private railcar. As the Windsors sat in their private limousine, waiting for the train, Lauder and her husband pulled up alongside in their car. Lauder approached the Windsors and said, "Oh, you are taking the train also."[5] A photographer had been tipped off to the "chance meeting," and photographs of Lauder and the royal couple appeared in newspapers the next day. Lauder joined them for the two-day trip to New York City. It was the beginning of a lasting friendship.

FAMOUS FRIENDS

Lauder had many famous friends during her lifetime, including Monaco's Princess Grace, former First Lady Nancy Reagan, and the matriarch of the Kennedy family, Rose Kennedy. Rose Kennedy once introduced Lauder to her son, US Senator Ted Kennedy, as the woman who kept her beautiful. Other famous women, including Raisa Gorbachev, the wife of the president of the Soviet Union, and Princess Diana, asked to meet her when they visited the United States.

CHAPTER
NINE

AN AMAZING LIFE

After 50 years in the cosmetics business, Lauder never lost her passion for changing women's looks and experimenting with the possibilities of makeup. As the 1980s approached, she still attended every new Estée Lauder product launch. "I have never worked a day in my life without selling," she said.[1] Even though her son Leonard was in charge of the company's day-to-day operations, Lauder still worked to maintain the company she founded. She personally tried all the products to make sure they met her high standards.

Lauder had reached a legendary stature in the beauty industry and on the social scene. She was known internationally. Fashion-conscious women everywhere sought her opinions, and beauty magazine editors loved to interview her. Her company continued to grow, and to her delight, her grandchildren developed a genuine interest in the business. It was always Lauder's goal to keep the business in the family. She believed her family was the heart and soul of the business and nobody could

Lauder and her husband enjoyed an active social life into their seventies.

care as much about it as members of her own family. Most important, she believed her family would share her concern about the quality of Estée Lauder products.

A STRONG LEGACY

Today, the company Estée Lauder founded sells products in 150 countries and territories. Its 28 brands include Estée Lauder and Clinique, as well as fragrance and cosmetic lines for Donna Karan, Tommy Hilfiger, Bobbi Brown, and Tom Ford. The company has more than 21,000 employees worldwide and is worth an estimated $10 billion. Estée Lauder products account for an amazing 45 percent of all cosmetics sales in department stores.

The company went public in 1995 as The Estée Lauder Companies, raising more than $450 million through initial stock offerings. Lauder wanted the company to remain privately held, but agreed to go public when she was promised her family would hold on to a vast majority of the stock. The family controls approximately 65 percent of the stock. Leonard Lauder is chairman emeritus and Ronald Lauder is chairman of Clinique Laboratories. Estée's grandson William, Leonard's son, is executive chairman. Another grandson, Gary, Leonard's younger son, chose not to be in the business. He is the managing partner of an investment firm in Silicon Valley, California. Ronald's daughters are also key executives: Aerin is senior vice president/creative director for Estée Lauder and Jane is global president and general manager of the Origins and Ojon brands. Both of Lauder's daughters-in-law joined the business. Leonard's wife, Evelyn, whom he married in 1959, served as a senior corporate vice president. Ronald and Jo Carole were married in 1967. Jo Carole worked with her husband to develop the Clinique line.

A Sudden Loss

Though Lauder always seemed ready to take on any challenge, on January 15, 1983, her world changed forever. She and Joseph were attending a family dinner at the Manhattan home of their son Ronald. The dinner was a celebration of their fortieth wedding anniversary. Joseph, who was 80 years old, had been ill earlier in the week but was now feeling better. As the couple prepared to leave the dinner at around midnight, Joseph collapsed. He was taken to a nearby hospital but pronounced dead on arrival.

Estée was grief stricken following Joseph's sudden death. She stayed away from the office, though Leonard still consulted with her. She toned down her active social life as well. She was seen at a few Broadway shows and some parties, but for the most part she kept out of the public eye. Lauder might have maintained her low profile had it not been for news she received in 1984. Author Lee Israel was writing an unauthorized biography about her.

Throughout her career,
Lauder was known for giving
out tidbits of useful advice
about beauty, business, and
life in general. These nuggets
of wisdom became known
as *Lauderisms*. For instance,
"Beauty is an attitude," she
once said. "There's no secret.
Why are all brides beautiful?
Because on their wedding
day they care about how
they look. There are no ugly
women—only women who
don't care or who don't
believe they're attractive."3
Another Lauderism: "Take
good care of your face. You
only have one."4

Just the Facts

Throughout most of her life, few facts about Lauder were made available to the public. Her upbringing, place of birth, dates of her marriage and remarriage, when her children were born, and even her own age were all kept secret from the public. Her son Leonard was once asked his age for an article. Leonard replied, "My age? I'll have to ask my mother. Every time she gives an interview, I'm a different age. I'll check on what I am this week and let you know."2

Lauder developed fanciful tales about her upbringing. When meeting new people, she suggested she grew up in Viennese palaces and had aristocratic blood running through her veins. She almost never acknowledged her Jewish heritage, though her husband and son always did. When Joseph died, his obituary did not even include his

Lauder returned to public life in the mid-1980s.

BETTER WITH AGE

Lauder never lost her passion for selling behind the counter. When she was in her seventies and early eighties, she would often go to a department store near her New York town house and get behind the counter to sell. She wanted to be in the middle of the action. Not everyone recognized her. Ronald Lauder remembers his mother diligently working with one particular customer. When the sale was completed, the woman Lauder was helping turned to her and said, "You are a wonderful salesperson. I will recommend you to Estée Lauder."[5]

age. It just said he was in his seventies. It gave no birth or marriage dates.

Some said the mystery surrounding Lauder's life was a good marketing ploy. Hints of being born into an upper-class family and sharing the beauty secrets from that elegant society were good for business. In reality, her parents were not poor, but she always wished she had come from high society. Lauder was not the only beauty mogul to be tight-lipped about her age and background. Helena Rubinstein and Elizabeth Arden were not forthcoming with their personal information, either.

Not to be outdone, Lauder decided to write her own autobiography and beat Lee Israel to the punch. She promised to tell all—except for her age. She acknowledged in the book she has always managed to keep her age a secret. Lauder said women could be beautiful and stylish at any age, so she reasoned her age did not matter. She added, "Even if age did matter, for the record, I wouldn't tell you."[6] Lee Israel eventually found records to confirm Lauder's birth date as July 1, 1908, and her place of birth as Corona, Queens. Lauder's family later said she was born in 1906 but offered no proof.

Lauder rushed to write her autobiography, titled *Estée: A Success Story*. She completed the manuscript in four months. She was very forthright in the book, talking about all aspects of her life. She even admitted being ashamed of her parents' heavy European accents, though she loved them very much. She said part of the embarrassment was because she wanted to be 100 percent American. Lauder's book did not contain much

THERE FOR OTHERS

Estée Lauder Companies and the Lauder family support many types of charities, including the arts, environmental concerns, and health issues. The company is actively working to end breast cancer, raising millions of dollars for research. This effort was spearheaded by Lauder's daughter-in-law Evelyn. In 1992, Evelyn, a breast cancer survivor, helped develop the international symbol for breast cancer awareness—the pink ribbon.

At the same time, the Lauders have come under scrutiny for their efforts to use charitable deductions to avoid some federal taxes. In particular, Ronald Lauder has been criticized for taking aggressive advantage of tax breaks and loopholes available only to the ultra-rich to avoid millions of dollars in taxes.

Lauder made one of her last major public appearances in 1993 with her son Ronald. Throughout her life, she focused on family, fashion, and hard work.

chronological data, further concealing her age. Lee Israel's book, *Estée Lauder: Beyond the Magic*, did include dates and places in Lauder's life not publicly known before that, including her date and place of birth. Other than the inclusion of dates, the books did not differ substantially in their accounts of Lauder's life. Both books came out in October 1985.

With the publication of her autobiography, Lauder returned to public life. She held book signings and gave interviews. She dedicated the book to her late husband, Joseph. Lauder remained active until 1994, when she broke her hip. After that, she was rarely seen in public, but reports said she remained involved in business decisions. In 1998, *Time* magazine named her one of the 20 most influential business geniuses of the 1900s. She was the only woman to make the list. She had become one of the wealthiest self-made women in America, with a personal worth of $233 million.

A Glittering Memorial

On April 24, 2004, Estée Lauder died in her Upper East Side home at the age of 95. On May 10, a memorial service was held at the New York State Theatre at Lincoln Center in Manhattan. More than 2,400

Lauder was a longtime friend of television journalist Barbara Walters.

mourners attended. The New York Pops played a
prelude. Renowned violinist Itzhak Perlman performed
as well. Many well-known figures, including New
York governor George Pataki, New York City mayor
Michael Bloomberg, and renowned newswoman Barbara
Walters, all spoke at the service. So did her sons and
grandchildren. It was the type of event—glamorous,
star-studded, and family-oriented—Lauder herself
would have loved.

Everyone who spoke remembered a strong, intelligent, confident woman who once said, "If you love to work, and you have a goal, you'll get there. I didn't get there by wishing for it or hoping for it or dreaming about it.... I got there by working for it."[7]

TIMELINE

1908
Josephine Esther Mentzer is born in Corona, Queens, New York, on July 1.

1924
John Schotz, Estee's uncle and a chemist, opens his own business.

1927
Estée meets Joseph Lauter.

1930
Estée marries Joseph Lauter in New York City, New York, on January 15.

1933
Estée and Joseph have their first child, Leonard, on March 19.

1937
Estée and Joseph change the spelling of their last name from Lauter to Lauder.

1939

Estée and Joseph divorce on April 11.

1942

Estée and Joseph remarry on December 7.

1944

The Lauders' second child, Ronald,
is born on February 26.

1946

The Estée Lauder Company is founded in New York City.

1948

Estée Lauder gets counter space at Saks
Fifth Avenue in New York City.

1950

Estée Lauder gets counter space at
Neiman Marcus in Dallas, Texas.

1953

Youth Dew bath oil is launched.

TIMELINE

1958
Leonard Lauder joins his parents' company.

1960
Estée Lauder products expand into fashionable department stores in Europe.

1962
The "Lauder woman" debuts.

1965
Estée Lauder releases the Aramis line of products for men.

1968
The Clinique line is launched.

1972
Leonard Lauder becomes president of the Estée Lauder Company.

1983
Joseph Lauder dies suddenly on January 15.

1985
Estée publishes her autobiography,
Estée: A Success Story.

1994
Estée breaks her hip and withdraws from public life.

1995
Estée Lauder Companies Inc. goes public.

2004
Estée Lauder dies in her Manhattan home on April 24.

ESSENTIAL FACTS

Date of Birth
July 1, 1908

Place of Birth
Corona, Queens, New York

Date of Death
April 24, 2004

Parents
Rose and Max Mentzer

Education
Newtown High School, Corona, Queens

Marriage
Joseph Lauter (January 15, 1930). Divorced in 1939 and remarried December 7, 1942.

Children
Leonard, Ronald

Career Highlights
A strong-minded businesswoman, Estée Lauder was selling products in the most exclusive department stores by the end of the 1940s. She released Youth Dew bath oil and perfume in 1953, which put her company on the road to $1 million in sales by 1958. Her company also went international in 1960.

Lauder became one of the most successful self-made women in American history.

Societal Contributions

Estée Lauder showed women her vision of beauty and then helped them attain it. Lauder pioneered marketing techniques and set an example for women who wanted to become successful entrepreneurs. Additionally, her company has donated millions of dollars to a variety of charities.

Conflicts

Estée Lauder was one woman against an industry of successful corporations that tried to squeeze out any newcomers. Yet Lauder would not be denied. She approached exclusive department stores that already had full cosmetics counters, convincing store managers she had a product people wanted.

Quote

"If you love to work, and you have a goal, you'll get there. I didn't get there by wishing for it or hoping for it or dreaming about it.... I got there by working for it." —*Estée Lauder*

GLOSSARY

aura
A quality or characteristic that surrounds a person or object.

bespectacled
Wearing glasses.

cachet
Prestige.

catered
Accommodated to needs or requirements.

complexion
The color, texture, and general appearance of a person's skin.

coveted
Desperately wanted.

crossover sale
The boosting of sales of all products in a line when one of them does well.

dermatologist
A doctor who treats skin conditions.

extolling
Praising.

fray
A situation involving intense competition.

hypoallergenic
Designed to prevent allergic reactions.

mogul
A successful business owner or entrepreneur.

ravishing
Beautiful to the point of being entrancing.

rue
Regret.

scoffing
Mocking and ridiculing.

stalwart
A leader or established figure.

stock
A small share in a company that is available for purchase by anyone.

waned
Diminished.

ADDITIONAL RESOURCES

Selected Bibliography

Israel, Lee. *Estée Lauder: Beyond the Magic*. New York: Macmillan, 1985. Print.

Lauder, Estée. *Estée: A Success Story*. New York: Random, 1985. Print.

Peiss, Kathy. *Hope in a Jar: The Making of America's Beauty Culture*. New York: Holt, 1999. Print.

Further Readings

Buchholz, Todd. *New Ideas from Dead CEOs: Lasting Lessons from the Corner Office*. New York: Harper, 2007. Print.

Koehn, Nancy F. *Brand New: How Entrepreneurs Earned Consumers' Trust from Wedgwood to Dell*. Boston: Harvard Business School, 2001. Print.

Schweitzer, Marlis. *When Broadway was the Runway: Theater, Fashion and American Culture*. Philadelphia, PA: U of Pennsylvania P, 2009. Print.

Web Sites

To learn more about Estée Lauder, visit ABDO Publishing Company on the World Wide Web at **www.abdopublishing.com**. Web sites about Estée Lauder are featured on our Book Links page. These links are routinely monitored and updated to provide the most current information available.

Places to Visit

Fashion Institute of Design & Merchandising (FIDM)
919 South Grand Avenue
Los Angeles, California 90015
213-623-5821
http://fidmmuseum.org/collections/fragrance
The FIDM features the only museum of its kind in the United States, the Annette Green Fragrance Archive, which focuses on the history of fragrances dating back to the 1880s. The exhibit contains perfume bottles, advertising and packaging through the years, as well as historical accounts of the fragrance industry and perfume-related memorabilia.

Estée Lauder Stores
1-877-311-3883
http://www.esteelauder.com/locator/index.tmpl
To see Lauder's products in person, find a store near you. Some include spas with special makeover rooms. Customers are given personal attention the way Estée Lauder provided it in her early days working behind the counter.

National Museum of American Jewish History
101 South Independence Mall East
Philadelphia, Pennsylvania 19106
215-923-3811
http://www.nmajh.org
The museum includes a display on Estée Lauder, as well as other important figures in American Jewish history.

SOURCE NOTES

Chapter 1. Youth Dew

1. Estée Lauder. *Estée: A Success Story*. New York: Random, 1985. Print. 77.

2. Joan Juliet Buck. "Estée Lauder: Face to Face." *Vogue* Jan. 1986: 268. Print.

3. Estée Lauder. *Estée: A Success Story*. New York: Random, 1985. Print. 78.

4. Ibid. 82.

5. Scranton, Philip. *Beauty and Business: Commerce, Gender, and Culture in Modern America*. New York: Routledge, 2001. Print. 235.

6. Estée Lauder. *Estée: A Success Story*. New York: Random, 1985. Print. 24–25.

Chapter 2. Growing Up Beautiful

1. Joan Juliet Buck. "Estée Lauder: Face to Face." *Vogue* Jan. 1986: 267. Print.

2. Estée Lauder. *Estée: A Success Story*. New York: Random, 1985. Print. 8.

3. Ibid. 9.

4. Ibid. 18.

5. Ibid. 12.

Chapter 3. A Fresh Face

1. Estée Lauder. *Estée: A Success Story*. New York: Random, 1985. Print. 19–20.

2. "Estée Lauder: The Sweet Smell of Success." *Entrepreneur*. Entrepreneur Media, 10 Oct. 2008. Web. 8 Mar. 2013.

Chapter 4. Life Lessons

1. Estée Lauder. *Estée: A Success Story*. New York: Random, 1985. Print. 31.

2. Ibid. 4.

3. Ibid. 3.

4. Veronica Horwell. "Estée Lauder." *Guardian*. Guardian News and Media Limited, 27 Apr. 2004. Web. 8 Mar. 2013.

5. Richard Severo. "Estée Lauder, Pursuer of Beauty and Cosmetics Titan, Dies at 97." *New York Times*. New York Times, 26 Apr. 2004. Web. 8 Mar. 2013.

6. David Patrick Columbia. "The List: In Memoriam." *David Patrick Columbia's New York Social Diary*. David Patrick Columbia & Jeffrey Hirsch, 11 May 2004. Web. 8 Mar. 2013.

7. Estée Lauder. *Estée: A Success Story*. New York: Random, 1985. Print. 36.

Chapter 5. Expanding the Brand

1. Estée Lauder. *Estée: A Success Story*. New York: Random, 1985. Print. 54.

2. Joan Juliet Buck. "Estée Lauder: Face to Face." *Vogue* Jan. 1986: 268. Print.

Chapter 6. Gaining More Ground

1. Lee Israel. *Estée Lauder: Beyond the Magic*. New York: Macmillan, 1985. Print. 48.

2. Estée Lauder. *Estée: A Success Story*. New York: Random, 1985. Print. 43.

3. Lee Israel. *Estée Lauder: Beyond the Magic*. New York: Macmillan, 1985. Print. 48.

SOURCE NOTES CONTINUED

Chapter 7. Innovations
1. Lee Israel. *Estée Lauder: Beyond the Magic*. New York: Macmillan, 1985. Print. 48.
2. Estée Lauder. *Estée: A Success Story*. New York: Random, 1985. Print. 91.
3. Lee Israel. *Estée Lauder: Beyond the Magic*. New York: Macmillan, 1985. Print. 60–69.
4. Estée Lauder. *Estée: A Success Story*. New York: Random, 1985. Print. 129.
5. Ibid. 130.

Chapter 8. New Ventures
1. Lee Israel. *Estée Lauder: Beyond the Magic*. New York: Macmillan, 1985. Print. 63.
2. Tatiana Morales. "Cosmetics Mogul Estée Lauder Dies: Got Her Start Blending Face Creams in Kitchen; Died at 95." *CBS News*. Associated Press, 25 Apr. 2004. Web. 8 Mar. 2013.
3. Estée Lauder. *Estée: A Success Story*. New York: Random, 1985. Print. 139.
4. Nancy F. Koehn. *Brand New: How Entrepreneurs Earned Customers' Trust from Wedgwood to Dell*. Boston: Harvard Business School Publishing, 2001. Print. 196.
5. Lee Israel. *Estée Lauder: Beyond the Magic*. New York: Macmillan, 1985. Print. 67.

Chapter 9. An Amazing Life
1. Tatiana Morales. "Cosmetics Mogul Estée Lauder Dies: Got Her Start Blending Face Creams in Kitchen; Died

at 95." *CBS News*. Associated Press, 25 Apr. 2004. Web. 8 Mar. 2013.

2. Estée Lauder. *Estée: A Success Story*. New York: Random, 1985. Print. 7.

3. Tatiana Morales. "Cosmetics Mogul Estée Lauder Dies: Got Her Start Blending Face Creams in Kitchen; Died at 95." *CBS News*. Associated Press, 25 Apr. 2004. Web. 8 Mar. 2013.

4. Rachel Urquhart. "All in the Family." *Vogue* Sept. 1994: 424. Print.

5. A&E Biography. *Estée Lauder: Sweet Smell of Success*. Narrated by Martha Teichner; hosted by Harry Smith. New York: A&E Entertainment, 1999.

6. Estée Lauder. *Estée: A Success Story*. New York: Random, 1985. 7.

7. "Estée Lauder Dies at 97." *CBS News*. CBS News, 8 June 2004. Web. 8 Mar. 2013.

INDEX

free gifts, 46–47, 51, 53, 57, 58, 76
  samples, 14, 31, 38, 46, 47, 53
  word of mouth, 39–40
men's cosmetics, 66
Mentzer, Max, 18, 20, 28
Mentzer, Renee, 19
Mentzer, Rose, 17–19, 22
Morris, Florence, 32–33
mystery shoppers, 57

Neiman Marcus, 7, 47, 55–57
New York City, 7, 17–18, 29–30, 40, 41, 45, 60, 80, 83

Orentreich, Norman, 75

Plafker and Rosenthal, 20–22
prices, 11–12, 65, 68
product testing, 9, 75

Queens, New York, 17, 20, 27, 91

Re-Nutriv, 65–69
Revlon, 48, 66, 73, 77
Rosenthal, Abraham, 17–18
Rubinstein, Helena, 9, 30, 48, 58–60, 66, 67, 90

Saks Fifth Avenue, 7, 47–48, 51–53, 55, 69
saleswomen, 40–41, 50, 53, 57–58, 78
Schotz, John, 7, 23–25, 28
Skrebneski, Victor, 70

Vogue, 9, 70, 75, 76

Walters, Barbara, 38, 94
Windsor, Duchess of, 32, 81–83
World War I, 23
World War II, 36

Youth Dew, 7–15, 58–63, 65, 72

ABOUT THE AUTHOR

Robert Grayson is an award-winning former daily newspaper reporter and the author of more than a dozen books for young adults. Throughout his journalism career, Grayson has written profiles on professional athletes and notable business leaders, plus stories on arts & entertainment, business, politics, and pets.